ANGER MANAGEMENT STORIES FOR KIDS

A PARENT'S GUIDE TO EMPOWER AND HELP KIDS TO UNDERSTAND THEIR EMOTIONS AND TO HELP THEM CONTROL THEIR ANGER THROUGH FUN AND SHORT STORIES

SARA E.H.

CONTENTS

THE MAGIC MIRROR

Once upon a time, there was a little girl with big dreams; she wanted to grow up just like her Mommy and was always imagining herself as a grown-up.

One day, while browsing in an old curiosity shop looking for grown-up clothes, she found a magic mirror.

"It will show you the past," the shopkeeper whispered, "and it will show you the future. But you must never let anyone else look into it. It will show only *your* past and only *your* future."

Excited to see her future, the little girl bought the mirror. She wrapped it up to keep it secret, took it home, tiptoed to her messy bedroom, and hid it under her unmade bed.

That night, she took it out, leaned it against her wall, looked into it, and asked it a question.

"Can you show me what I will look like when I grow up?" she asked.

Her reflection began to swirl and turned into a very pretty grown-up, wearing very pretty grown-up clothes. The little girl looked at her in awe.

But then the grown-up looked around the girl's messy room and wagged her finger angrily.

Embarrassed, the little girl cried and immediately put the mirror back under the bed.

The next night, she tried again, and just like before, her grown-up reflection got angry and wagged her finger at the child. This time, the child also got angry and told her grown-up reflection she hated her, hated the mirror, and never wanted to see her again. And then she put the mirror away and never took it out again.

From then on, she never wanted to be a grown-up and always behaved like a naughty girl.

Many years passed, and the little girl really did grow up. She got a job and had a family of her own. Her children were a handful; she always felt tired, constantly cleaning up after them.

One day, out of curiosity, she visited her old home, looked around her old room, and found the magic mirror still under the bed after all these years.

She took it out, leaned it against the wall, looked into it, and asked it a question.

"Can you show me what I looked like as a child?"

Her reflection began to swirl, and she saw it turn into a pretty little girl wearing a pretty little dress, looking back at her in awe.

But her room was so messy that, out of habit from constantly having to tidy up after her own kids, she wagged her finger and told her young self to tidy her room. The child immediately began to cry, and the mirror went dark.

Disappointed, she tried again.

"Show me what I looked like when I was a child."

Sure enough, her reflection began to swirl again, and she saw it turn into a child again. This time, she was scowling and angry.

"I hate you, and hate the mirror, and never want to see you again," said the child.

But this time, the grown-up girl crouched, came close to the mirror, and spoke softly.

"I understand why you are upset, and it's normal to feel that way."

The child softened her frown.

"Do you want a hug?" the grown-up asked, "And then we can tidy up together?"

The child nodded.

And the two reached through the magic mirror and hugged.

The book you are holding in your hands right now is, in some ways, like a magic mirror. Just as Gandhi famously said, "Be the change you want to see in the world." I believe that, as parents, we can be the change we want to see in our *children* because in many ways, they are a reflection of us, and their temperaments a reflection of ours.

I will never forget when my daughter, at age three, stared at the crashed computer, slapped the mouse on the desk, and said with precocious frustration, "Urgh, I hate this f@%#ing computer!"

Guilty as charged.

But it's not all bad news and mitigating the negatives; the magic mirror works both ways.

While taking a break from writing this book, watering the plants in the backyard, I noticed a dragonfly suffering in the Texas summer heat. After calling my kids to look at the precious thing, we placed it in the shade on a leaf floating in a bowl of water. After updating the girls the following day that the dragonfly had passed away, my youngest responded with layers of insight.

"You did a kind thing," she said. "We have to be kind, even to mean people, to teach them how to be nice."

I wanted to be kind to the dragonfly and, like most parents, wanted to use the moment as a teaching opportunity. This was doubly rewarding: My daughter did not simply see the obvious lesson that being kind is the right thing to do. She saw the deeper lesson—the true reflection of my intention—that acts of kindness can guide others who may not know better. She saw my intention and mirrored it.

If we consider the impact of this "pay it forward" idea, of guiding our children to become not just good people but good *teachers* of people, and accept they are innately wired to reflect our intentions, we should then recognize that the opportunities, as well as the responsibilities and rewards, are enormous.

This is a book to help parents and children alike share what frustrates us as well as what inspires us, and find the right path together. This book is an invitation to reach through the magic mirror and hug our reflection.

Through simple parables, short stories, and games, this book will present a few common traps we may sometimes fall into—in story form understandable to children and adults alike—and offer some helpful guidance on navigating them. Following each story will be a few questions and talking points so that, when read to kids, the lessons can be *discovered by* rather than *preached to* them.

We will back up the messages with tried and tested practices, psychology, and science to ensure you and your child have more tools to get through the day.

We hope you develop a bond through storytelling that can generate a common understanding—a common *language*—that is both personal and healthy. Here's an example of how it worked for me:

When my second child was born, my first became jealous and started to act out. I read some books on sibling jealousy, learned the core message they all taught, and then wrote a story called "The Orchid and the Cactus" for her.

The story was about a gardener who collected flowers from around the world and tended them as they needed to be tended. But soon, the cactus, who needed sun and sand and not much else, became jealous of the new arrival, the orchid, who needed constant watering. When the cactus confronted the gardener, asking if he loved orchids more than cacti, he said he loved all his flowers equally but differently.

"I love each flower as it needs to be loved," he explained. "That is my job as a gardener."

I was shocked at how effective it was. After I finished writing the story and read it to my daughter, her response was, "Am I the cactus?"

She was correct; she was. Older and stronger, needing only sunlight and sand to thrive, the cactus would have died if watered like the orchid. And after that, whenever she became jealous, I'd ask, "Who are you?"

"I'm the cactus."

"And what do you need?"

"Sun and sand."

"Who is your baby sister?"

"She's the orchid."

"And what does she need?"

"Shade and water."

"Do you want me to give you shade and water?"

"No."

"Are you still jealous?"

"No."

It worked.

And the lesson for me was that, in telling children's stories and helping them discover for themselves the life lessons hidden within them, my kids found their own way.

I hope these stories and exercises work for your family, too.

THE MAGIC MIRROR

```
R G N B E D R O O M
O D I C H H C U V Q
O A Q R L U L N L F
M I V M L G E D T A
D R E S S P A P U N
M I R R O R N R P G
J T S W X E I E S R
M A G I C D N T E Y
H B E D P B G T T A
B E H A V E V Y N H
```

cleaning	bedroom	mirror	girl
behave	magic	angry	bed
dress	upset	hug	
pretty	room		

THE ORCHID AND THE CACTUS

```
C B J X O R C H I D
T H R I V E Q J P F
S S L C L X F E B L
A M I O A C W A A O
N A G S V C A L B W
D T S S T E T O Y E
K C Y H L E E U B R
S I M W A K R S S S
U R D Q K D R J F Y
N I I S Q C E A U C
```

jealous   flowers   orchid   sand

cactus   thrive   sister   love

shade   water   kids   sun

baby

HOW TO USE THIS BOOK

In the following pages, we will walk together through what I believe are the essential steps to finding peace with your child.

The first step is to get their permission to proceed. Because without that, good luck.

Each chapter will begin with an introduction for the parent's eyes, to better understand the chapter's objective.

Then follows a story, fable, or game that should be read to or played with your child.

After that, I recommend a few talking points to allow your child to think about the meaning of the story.

Throughout the book, your child will be gently guided to consider themes of frustration and emotional expression and to deduce for themselves how to advise the characters in the story. Indirectly, they will be considering:

- How their anger may not be in their best interests
- How to accept that their innate programming is not their fault
- How to identify, label, and recognize heightened emotions
- How to imagine breaking free from impulsive behavior
- How to avoid getting baited
- How empathy can free them from frustration

And just like with my daughter and the story of the orchid and the cactus, by developing a common language, you and your child will soon get on the same page.

I wish you and your family well and look forward to hearing about your experiences.

DON'T GET BY; GET BUY-IN

THE SETUP

If there is one thing I have learned in life, it's that we cannot make someone do something with any degree of conviction if they do not *want* to do it. The best way to have someone open themselves to learning new skills is first to get their buy-in. Only when they have signed up and agreed to play along can the effective work begin.

If this book is to be effective in opening up a dialogue between ourselves and our child, we will need to have our child *want* to play the game. The following story aims to get their buy-in.

If we read this story to our child and talk about it afterward using the prompts at the end of this section, we should be able to get them to want to play.

ALFRED AND ROMEO

On either side of a hedge that separated two backyards sat two dogs. Alfred was confident and protective, proud and strong. Romeo was softer, quieter, and more laid-back.

When their owners were around, Alfred and Romeo sat, rolled over, chased tennis balls, slept, and did all the usual things dogs do. But after the owners left for work or school, Alfred and Romeo went to the backyard, sat by the hedge, and chatted—usually about food.

And this sunny Monday morning was no different.

"Morning, Alfred," said Romeo, peering through the hedge.

"Morning, Romeo," said Alfred, peering back.

"What did you have for breakfast this morning?" Romeo inquired.

"Dog food," Alfred replied, a bit bored with the menu.

"Yeah, me too," Romeo agreed, "and then I had a bone."

"They give you bones?" Alfred was annoyed. "How come I never get bones?"

Romeo was just about to answer when they both heard a banging at the front door of Alfred's house.

"Attack!!!" Alfred yelled. "I'm being attacked. I gotta go."

At that, Alfred started barking and yelling and ran indoors towards the front door. The attacker was now trying to enter through the letterbox, and Alfred fumed, scratched, and snarled from inside, trying to scare him away.

It worked.

Alfred was a bit shaken but proud that he had stood his ground and prevented what could have been a terrible human attack. He returned to the backyard, sat by the hedge, and picked up the conversation where they had left off.

"That showed him," he boasted to Romeo. "Anyway, where were we? Bones…"

Just then, they both heard banging again, this time coming from Romeo's front door.

"Dude, now YOU are being attacked!" Alfred insisted. "Are you going to defend yourself?"

But Romeo didn't move.

"No," Romeo replied and was just about to explain why not when Alfred went ballistic on his behalf and stopped listening to reason.

"Well," Alfred insisted. "I'm gonna let him know I'm watching him." And at that, Alfred started barking, growling, and running around in circles in the backyard until he was exhausted. After that, they both agreed it was probably time for a nap.

On Tuesday, the same thing happened. They met at the hedge and discussed breakfast, and Alfred got annoyed about Romeo's bone. Then Alfred's house was attacked, and Alfred scared the attacker away. Then Romeo's house was attacked, and Romeo ignored him. Then Alfred ran around in circles, all riled up. And then they napped.

Wednesday was a little different. They met a bit earlier than usual this time and started the usual conversation.

"Morning, Alfred," said Romeo.

"Morning, Romeo," said Alfred.

"Breakfast?" Romeo inquired.

"Dog food," Alfred replied. "Please don't tell me you had bones again. It's making me angry."

"Well," Romeo began, "I tried to tell you. Every time the butcher comes around, putting bones through the mail slot for all the local dogs, you scare him away. If you weren't so defensive, he might have a chance to push a bone through the door for you."

Just then, they heard a banging at Alfred's door. Romeo watched through the hedge as Alfred struggled to contain his instincts to defend himself. He growled, snarled under his breath, and shook angrily, but he didn't run at the door; he managed to control himself, hoping that the bone man would leave him a bone.

On Thursday morning, the two met up again.

"Morning, Alfred," said Romeo.

"Morning, Romeo," said Alfred.

"Breakfast?" Romeo inquired.

Alfred smiled. "Bones."

Just then, they heard a banging at Alfred's door.

"Aren't you going to get that?" Romeo asked.

"Nope," Alfred replied before going back to chewing on his bone.

THE CHATTERBOX

Here are a few suggested talking points for you and your child to discuss.

1. Which dog did you relate to? Alfred or Romeo?
2. Why did you relate to him?
3. Why do you think Alfred wanted to scare the bone man away?
4. Do you ever feel like you need to defend yourself by being angry?
5. Can you be sure you know who is knocking on your door and why they are knocking?
6. Would it have been better for Alfred if he had waited to see or understand what the bone man was doing?

7. What do you think is the better approach for Alfred next time someone knocks at his door?
8. Did you like this story?
9. Would you like us to read more together?

ALFRED AND ROMEO

```
G H Y E L L I N G D
C D T J I K E P H L
O A E M S S X R S S
N N G F T K H O T T
F N R Q E E A U R R
I O O F N N U D O U
D Y W B I E S N N G
E E L O N H T I G G
N D M N G T E I V L
T Z T E C U D S V E
```

listening	defensive	exhausted
yelling	annoyed	strong
struggle	confident	growl
proud	bone	

4

REPROGRAMMING THE TEMPER-BOT

THE SETUP

As much as we would like to think of ourselves as rational—and to some degree, we are—we are also emotional. I could start talking about parts of the brain, adrenaline, and psychological mumbo jumbo, but I won't (yet). When dealing with an emotionally heightened situation, none of that matters. Academics can do that work. Our job, as parents, is on the front line, helping our kids. Mumbo jumbo won't help.

Tantrums, anger outbursts, and shouting are primal reactions to perceived threats. These responses are almost programmed into us, one way or another. When someone makes us jump, we don't think "That masked person just scared me, so I think the best thing for me to do is jump and scream." No. We do it without thinking. And if we are to help our children, it starts with a reassurance that they are doing what they are programmed to do.

This primal response, known to many as the "fight or flight" response, comes from a particular part of the brain. Oh, I promised not to talk about that, didn't I? Anyway, it's like a rapid-response call center, not a considered reply; it's a quick response with a limited palette of options—like a fast-food menu. When a lion jumped out of hiding in front of our ancestors, those who survived the threat of becoming fast food themselves and went on to have us were the ones whose survival instincts acted quickly, the ones who fought back or fled: Fight or flight.

While we can't undo a million years of evolutionary programming, we *can* "use our words" to help our child label these responses so that we can refer to them when they happen again.

We may not be as strong as a lion, but we are great with words, which puts us at an advantage. Words will get us through this in the form of a patch for our programming to circumvent our instincts.

The following story may provide some objectivity for your child. Read it to them and then follow with a quick chat using the prompts in the chatterbox.

BILLY'S DOG-MATIC

In the not-too-distant future, robot pets will become commonplace. And it is in a robot pet shop, twenty years from now, that our story takes place.

In the future pet shop, the F-Series dog-matics will have become the must-have accessory. Every kid will either have one or *have* to have one, and on Billy's 5th birthday, it was time to go shopping for his very own F-series dog-matic.

Dog-matics were fully computerized, carbon-coated, static-resistant, mechanical, automatic dogs available in every shape and size. And the F-series was the newest version. The E-series were lovely dog-matics designed to be the perfect human companion. But they could sometimes be very emotional. They could whine, cry, or become sad or fearful. And while these emotions were necessary for all dog-matics, some tended to cry all day or mope around. So, scientists adjusted the programming and made the dog-matics stronger.

Or so they thought.

In making them stronger, the scientists overlooked one important thing; the dog-matics still had emotions—they didn't go away—but now they just hid their upset and fears by behaving differently. In every other way, these F-series dog-matics were perfect, and in fact, the shopkeeper showed Billy the different ways each dog-matic reacted to being fearful so he could pick the one he liked the most.

"Billy," the shopkeeper said, "I want to show you five different F-series dog-matics, okay?"

"Okay," said Billy.

"They each respond differently if scared," the shopkeeper explained, "and to simulate this, all you have to do is pull this trigger."

The shopkeeper handed a small box to Billy. It had five little switches, or triggers, as the shopkeeper called them.

"When I introduce you to each dog-matic, I want you to play with it and then press their trigger, okay?"

"Okay," said Billy.

"Good," said the shopkeeper. "The first dog-matic is called Fightsie."

Fightsie bounded out of bed and started licking Billy, and in turn, Billy tickled her belly. Fightsie rolled over, sat on command, and was perfect. Billy loved Fightsie and wanted to take her home.

"I want Fightsie," said Billy.

"But you haven't triggered her yet," the shopkeeper reminded him.

So, Billy flipped the first switch and triggered Fightsie.

Immediately, Fightsie crouched and growled, snarled, and barked.

"No, no," said Billy, shocked by the change in her behavior. "Make her stop." And he quickly turned off the trigger.

But this didn't stop Fightsie from growling and barking, and in the end, Fightsie had to be taken back to her bed to calm down on her own.

"Why did she do that?" Billy asked. "And why didn't she stop?"

"When she feels afraid, she thinks she needs to fight back," the shopkeeper explained. "And it takes her some time to calm down."

"OK, then I'm not so sure about her," admitted Billy. "Who's next?"

"Next up is Flighty," said the shopkeeper. And out came the next dog-matic: Flighty.

Flighty was perfect and playful until he was triggered. As soon as Billy flipped the switch, simulating fear, Flighty turned and ran right out the door, and he never came back, even after Billy turned off the trigger.

"Once triggered," the shopkeeper explained, "it takes time for him to calm down. He tends to run away from fear. Don't worry; I think you will like the next one. This dog-matic is called Floppsie."

Floppsie was just as friendly as Fightsie and Flighty, and Billy giggled a lot when tickling her. But when triggered, Floppsie went, well, all floppy. She just didn't do anything. When Billy tried to tickle or play with her in any way, Floppsie didn't play.

Pretty soon, Billy realized Floppsie wasn't so much fun after all.

"Not a problem," said the shopkeeper. "She thinks going soft and small will make her safer. It is good that we are testing these. Next up, I think you are going to love him. His name is Freezie."

Freezie bounded up, licked Billy, sat, and rolled over, just like the others. But when triggered, he immediately froze. He stood still, staring at Billy, seemingly terrified.

Billy switched the trigger back to the off position and hugged Freezie. But Freezie stayed frozen.

The shopkeeper reminded Billy that when dog-matics are triggered, it usually takes time for them to calm down.

"It's normal," he added. "He just doesn't move. He is too frightened. It's like he is hiding by not moving."

Then the shopkeeper introduced Billy to the fifth and final dog-matic, Friendsie.

"Frenzy?" Billy asked, "Like, crazy? That doesn't sound good."

"No," the shopkeeper replied. "As in 'friend.' Friendsie."

Friendsie jumped up like all the others, rolled over, and loved having her back scratched.

Then Billy triggered Friendsie.

At first, Friendsie stepped back and raised her eyebrows. Little question marks appeared in her digital eyes, and she watched

Billy cautiously for a moment. But then she started wagging her tail and stepped closer to Billy. In return, Billy reached out and patted Friendsie and then scratched her back. It took a moment for Friendsie to return to her usual playful self, but they worked it out and eventually played happily again.

In fact, they were so playful that Billy forgot to un-trigger her. But that wasn't even necessary; the play had untriggered her naturally.

"When Friendsie is scared," the shopkeeper explained, "she uses her skills to engage with you. She befriends you."

But Billy wasn't listening; he was too busy tickling Friendsie.

"So, Billy," the shopkeeper concluded. "You have met all the F-series dog-matics; Fightsie, Flighty, Floppsie, Freezie, and Friendsie. Have you decided which one you want?"

"Yes, that one," said Billy, pointing to one of the dog-matics.

And at that, Billy and his new friend walked happily out the door.

THE CHATTERBOX

Here are a few suggested talking points for you and your child to discuss.

1. Which dog-matic do you think Billy picked: Fightsie, Flighty, Floppsie, Freezie, or Friendsie?
2. Which dog-matic would you have picked?
3. What did you think of each dog-matic's response to being scared?
4. Is there a dog-matic you relate to more than the others? Why?
5. Can you relate to the other reactions?
6. Have you ever fought back?
7. Have you ever run away?
8. What things feel like they upset you?
9. If you were a dog-matic, which one would you rather be? Why?

TEMPER-BOT

```
A M M T Z P U T P C A L M S V
F P A Y O C K S C A R E D L O
E B F N O Q D I Q Y V J T V S
A M J R G Q Y S D M X T E E X
R A E O F E N R O S P R N S C
F D N B K N R U B F R I M T V
U E M O T I O N A L T G C W G
L P S T M Y J C V T Y G B H J
S A A D N B E M P J W E S A Z
T R D A N V V N Q H U R W C Z
R E B T F O T E R R I F I E D
O N X L X R K X A W Y C T W S
N T F E T C A U T I O U S H L
G S Q R X F D I T A Y R Z Q Y
W N Z C S Y F F D Z I A M J L
```

emotional	terrified	cautious	soft
trigger	parents	fearful	kids
afraid	scared	anger	calm
strong	robot	run	sad

5

EMOTIONAL I-CUE

THE SETUP

Modern parenting is no different from parenting in any other era. Kids are kids. What is so powerful these days, however, is our access to resources. Understanding emotions was certainly not how I was raised, yet it is so prevalent today. And there is no shortage of resources for us to review. This is healthy progress.

It's an awful irony that as we research—probably on a computer or a phone—we exemplify the exact screen time behaviors that may frustrate us in our kids. (There's that magic mirror again.) But at least we are able to express our frustration when we feel it. If kids are not guided to use words to express emotions, they'll remain purely emotional, and that's a ticking time bomb.

A baby cries when it's hungry. It also cries when it is uncomfortable or tired. But by the time the child learns to say, "I'm hungry," crying becomes a "babyish" behavior they outgrow and even tease their peers about if it's displayed. (Though the crying may still occur if "Can I have more cookies" is met with "Finish your vegetables.")

When we accumulate such verbal skills, we kick the emotion tin can down the road. We are taught the word "hungry," and, in no time, crying is replaced by talking. We can continue to push back the "upset threshold"—raise their emotional IQ—by empowering our children with the right words to help them express their emotional hunger before the meltdown.

There are many commercially available emotional flashcards, or cue cards, that can help kids put labels on their feelings. The more they can express these feelings, the farther we push the tantrum threshold back, and the more we raise their emotional IQ. Mine is a "crafty" family, so we prefer to make our own cue cards. The more involved our child is, the more proud they tend to be. If you are not as crafty, any form of commercially available cue cards will help your child develop emotionally.

CHARADES

If we take a few key emotions, identify them, define them, provide examples of when we feel them, and draw pictures to illustrate them, we can create a custom set of our own emotional I-Cue cards that could benefit your child not only in the short term but, most critically, for the rest of their lives.

Start with the basic four emotions—happiness, sadness, fear, anger—and slowly build your collection. (The next four might be surprise, disgust, anticipation, and trust. A quick Google search is an easy way to find the wording that works best for you.)

Level 1: Read the emotion and its telltale traits until the child becomes familiar with them.

Level 2: Pick a card and read only the traits. See if your child can guess the emotion based on the characteristics alone.

Level 3: Pick a card and have your kid describe situations that make them feel that emotion. (e.g., Jealous: When my sister gets to stay up later than me.)

Level 4: Emotional mastery comes when playing Charades is easy. Someone picks a card and behaves and answers questions as if that is how they are feeling, without giving away the emotion. The other person has to guess what's going on.

By becoming skilled at identifying emotions, we kick the emotional can down the road; we push back their threshold of upset and raise their emotional IQ.

THE CHATTERBOX

Ideas to get the conversation started:

1. Can you list some emotions?
2. Which one do you find the hardest to deal with?
3. What causes you to feel that way?
4. Remember the dog-matics? Remember their "triggers"? Does it feel like sometimes you are provoked? Like, you can't control what made you start feeling that way?
5. What does it feel like when you are provoked?
6. What do you do when that emotion is triggered in you?
7. Remember Alfred and Romeo? What triggered Romeo?
8. What did Romeo do when he was triggered?
9. Are there things that trigger you? What are they?
10. When you are triggered into that feeling, what do you do?
11. Is that reaction more like Alfred or Romeo?
12. When you are angry, which dog-matic are you most like? Flighty? Fightsie? Friendsie?
13. Which dog-matic would you prefer to be?

Emotion Flashcards.

Print out the cards. Match the expression to an emotion.

EMOTIONS

We all have feelings. Our faces can tell others how we feel.
When we're happy, we smile, and when we're sad, we frown.
Look at the words below and write them in one of the boxes,
drawing that emotion on the blank face.

SAD HAPPY ANGRY SCARED

EMOTIONS

We all have feelings. Our faces can tell others how we feel. When we're happy, we smile, and when we're sad, we frown. Look at the words below and write them in one of the boxes, drawing that emotion on the blank face.

Excited Anxious Confused Calm

HOW ARE YOU FEELING?

Circle the correct feeling:

Happy   Anxious

Sad   Scared

HOW ARE YOU FEELING?

Circle the correct feeling:

Happy   Calm

Anxious   Tired

HOW ARE YOU FEELING?

Circle the correct feeling:

Excited   Sad

Angry   frightened

HOW ARE YOU FEELING?

Circle the correct feeling:

Mad   Scared

Excited   Sad

HOW ARE YOU FEELING?

Circle the correct feeling:

Confused   Angry

Excited   Happy

HOW ARE YOU FEELING?

Circle the correct feeling:

Scared   Sad

Angry   Happy

HOW ARE YOU FEELING?

Circle the correct feeling:

Frightened   Calm

Upset   Anxious

HOW ARE YOU FEELING?

Circle the correct feeling:

calm   Excited

Angry   confused

6

NO MORE PUPPETEERS

THE SETUP

I vividly recall when my eldest came home from school angry, complaining that she had gotten into trouble but that it was someone else's fault—as in, "They started it." How often do we blame others for our behavior? A lot is my guess.

I have a slightly contrarian view towards provocation— emotional versus physical hurt—and the right to say, "You made me feel…." In short, I believe we are responsible for our conduct, certainly physically, and in a more nuanced way, emotionally. We have no control over how we experience physical victimization. But with emotional victimization, at least we have options. Using our words, talking, and taking ownership of our internal processes are critical to developing healthy social and emotional habits.

I dislike the expression "You made me feel...." No one *makes* us feel. We cannot even make *ourselves* feel. We feel, *period*. And then we feel something *else*, and so on, perpetually riding the train of life and looking out the window at the stream of feelings whizzing by. Emotions are not *inflicted upon us* by others; they are internal experiences that *happen within* us in reaction to, well, whatever we see out the train window. Owning our emotional state, or at least not blaming it on others, is the ticket to emotional freedom.

A simple shift of words from "You made me feel..." to "When you did *XYZ*, I felt *ABC*..." may sound like semantics to some, but it sounds like ownership to our subconscious mind, where our messaging gets processed. Some believe that humans began to use language because we had well-developed brains. With zero qualification in this matter, I believe the opposite; we became so smart because we started to use language.

Words promote understanding.

When our children learn the words for emotions, they can start the journey of understanding themselves. And when they can frame the things that upset them in a way that accepts their internal workings are their own—their responsibility—they can move away from feeling victimized and towards mastery of self.

NO MORE PUPPETEERS

Mick and Finn were toys. They had been together for as long as they could remember. They recalled sitting together in the toy store. They remembered being picked up and taken to their forever home. And they loved when their owner used to play with them all the time.

These days, though, they didn't get played with as much, so they sat together and chatted about deep things like the meaning of life and emotions.

Mick was a toy man with the usual arms and legs, head and body, a face and hands.

Finn was a simpler toy. He still had arms, legs, and a head. But he didn't have fingers, a face, or toes. He was just a very floppy, simple, wooden figure. Mick could stand up. Finn couldn't, not on his own. He was just pieces of wood joined by string.

But just because he was a simple figure didn't mean he was a simple person. He was very emotional.

"I sometimes feel so upset," Finn admitted, "that I kick another toy."

"Yeah," said Mick, recalling the incident. "I know."

"She made me do it," Finn said. "And sometimes I feel upset, and I hit another toy."

"Yeah, I know that, too," said Mick.

"She made me do it," Finn said. "And then I feel horrible. She makes me feel horrible. Don't you ever feel like others make you do and feel things?" asked Finn.

"No," admitted Mick. "I mean, I have feelings, but no one *makes* me *feel* them. And when I do things, it's because *I* choose to. No one *controls* me."

"Wow," said Finn. "I can't imagine how that must be. I have such a cross to bear." And he started to cry.

"I have heard that expression before," Mick replied, a little confused. "Does it mean you are worried or feel bad?"

"No," said Finn, "I literally have a cross that I am attached to. Two, in fact. See these strings?"

Mick looked closely at Finn and saw some strings coming off his arms, legs, and head attached to sticks shaped like a cross.

"Oh," said Mick with a smile. "There's the problem."

Now it was Finn who was confused.

"How so?" he asked.

"I never noticed before," said Mick. "You're a puppet."

Finn was even more confused.

"Look," Mick explained. "When she picks up those sticks, she can control you. She pulls your strings, and you kick and hit. She can make you do things. She can make you feel things. You're her puppet. She pulls your strings."

"Isn't everyone like that?" asked Finn.

"No," replied Mick.

"Then who controls your body?"

"I do," said Mick.

"Who controls how you feel?"

"No one," Mick admitted, "so I can control how I act when I don't feel good."

"I don't want to be a puppet anymore," said Finn, wiping the puppet tears from his eyes. "I don't want her to make me do things I don't want to do."

"Okay," said Mick. "Let's cut those ties."

Mick and Finn got busy freeing Finn from all the strings. When they were done, Mick checked in.

"Are you a puppet?"

"No," said Finn.

"Does anyone control your body?"

"No," said Finn.

"Who controls your body?"

"I do," said Finn.

"And who controls your emotions?"

"No one," Finn replied, "so at least I can control how I act when I don't feel good."

"That's right." Mick nodded. "So, no more puppet tears?"

"That's right." Finn nodded. "No more puppeteers!"

THE CHATTERBOX

1. Who did you relate to in the story, Mick or Finn?
2. Do you sometimes feel someone makes you sad?
3. Do you sometimes feel someone makes you angry?
4. Do you sometimes do things when you are angry that you wouldn't do if you were not angry, like hitting, yelling, or breaking something?
5. Are you a puppet?
6. Does anyone have strings attached to you that make you do things?
7. Who controls your body?
8. Who is responsible for moving your arms and legs?

PUPPETEERS

```
T U N D E R S T A N D Q H X Z
J R Z W Y F S X A Q S I K U F
C M O U O O T V O D S A W P S
L O I U V R I U Y V D Y I S M
I W N Y B M R K F I R R Q E A
S W G F Y L A I Q W H K L T U
M K N T U V E H E I P E G P F
B S D I A S F C E D Y T S Z E
U T H B V A E P M M I C I Z E
M R U K C X P D G L Z O M J L
I I S M A R T Q L O W N P I I
F N L Q E Z X Q I V Y T L G N
F G T M R B Q W F E F R E T G
S S Y C B L A M E O M O X R S
O F S L Q O T Q G P A L F O H
```

understand	feelings	confused	love
control	worried	trouble	life
simple	strings	smart	
upset	blame		

7

HOW TO AVOID GETTING BAITED

THE SETUP

I have read many books on anger management, studied online, talked to other parents, and dived deep into how to better equip myself and my kids to deal with their emotional outbursts. But I think what opened my eyes the widest and gave me the most insight into navigating this path was my own kids.

I never regarded my kids as "just" kids; I regarded them as the same as everyone else, just with less life experience; apprentice adults, if you like. What's the difference? I am not sure exactly, but for me, it's a matter of respect. I related to their challenges, assumed they would get skilled once guided, and expected them to work with me to get there.

Studies support the idea that assuming identical intelligence, a class of kids who are told they are talented in a given subject and treated as such will achieve better grades than a class whose kids are treated as if they are less likely to succeed. When expectations are set high, kids tend to do better than when set low. And I recall, as a kid, when a teacher pointed out that I was particularly good at something, their confidence in me made me want to work harder. As a result, I did better.

Stating our expectations of our kids (even if they are a bit of a stretch) can start a self-fulfilling confidence loop, and I practiced it as much as possible. And one such opportunity was in self-regulation, being baited, and having empathy.

This chapter follows "Puppeteers" for a good reason. The first step to self-control mastery is the "what," or should I say, "what *not*." Practicing "what not" to do when emotions are heightened and taking responsibility for our actions is a huge step, but it's not the only one. Self-restraint can be an infuriating internal experience if we are the only ones "behaving," and if restraint becomes repression of emotions, that's unhealthy. But restraint—acting on the "what not"—gives us pause and space to consider the *"why."* And there is surely no concept more powerful when dealing with emotions—our own and those of the people around us—than understanding "why."

BE THE BIGGER FISH

Penny loved school, mostly.

Penny was a fish and went to a school of fish, where she learned to swim, hide, and play in the coral. She learned the names of other fish and plants and loved her friends.

But what she hated was the baiting.

Sometimes, worms would dive into the water, wriggle, and taunt the school of fish.

"They say mean things," Penny complained to her mom. "And if any of us ever get angry and bites back, there's a fight, the fish gets into trouble, and she gets taken out of school."

"They are baiting you," her mom said. "Don't take the bait. Be the bigger fish."

So Penny always tried to be the bigger fish. But it was frustrating. The worms always seemed to know what to say to upset her. And any time they called her a stupid minnow, Penny lost her temper.

Back at home, she talked with her mom.

"He called me a stupid minnow," Penny said.

"Hmm," pondered her mom. "Are you a stupid minnow?"

Penny was shocked by her question.

"Are you saying you think I am?" she asked, feeling her mom wasn't defending her against this mean accusation.

"No," her mom replied. "I'm asking you if you think you are. Because if you *are* a stupid minnow, he's *right*, and there's nothing to be angry about. And if you are *not*, he's *wrong*, and there's nothing to be angry about. I'm asking you if you think he is right or wrong."

"He's wrong," Penny said defiantly.

"Okay," her mom said. "So, what upset you?"

"He said mean things," said Penny, "and made other fish think mean things about me. He's lying."

Her mom pondered for a moment before responding.

"You know how, sometimes, you say I'm the best mom in the world?"

"Yes," Penny replied.

"Well, that's usually after I give you something you like, right?"

"Yes," Penny agreed.

"And sometimes, you say I am the *worst* mom in the world, right?"

"Yes," Penny agreed.

"That's usually after I have you do something you don't like, right?"

"Yes," Penny agreed.

"So, you have said that I am both the *best* mom in the world and the *worst*," she concluded. "But I can't be both, can I?"

"No," Penny agreed.

"What you say about me says less about *who I am*," she said, "and more about *how you feel*. You say nice things when you are happy and mean things when you are sad. I haven't changed, and neither have you; only your emotions have changed, and they affect what you say, right?"

Penny nodded.

"And it's the same when others say mean things to you," she said. "For them, it's not about *what others are*; it's about *how they feel*. No one else believes them when they say things like that. Don't take it personally. It's not about *you*; it's about *them* and how *they feel*. That doesn't make it okay for them to say it, of course, but it makes it a bit more understandable. And when you understand it, it's easier not to take it personally. So, try not to be baited. Understand that they are probably having a terrible day."

Penny nodded.

"And if you *really* want to be the bigger fish," she continued, "you could even try to understand *why* the worm is having a bad day."

So, Penny lay in her (sea) bed, at peace, knowing that the worm's words shouldn't be taken personally. They were probably said because the worm was having a bad day.

The next day, back at the school of fish, a worm turned up again, saying mean things and calling everyone a stupid minnow. Some other fish wanted to bite, but Penny stepped in.

"Stop," she said. "Maybe he's having a bad day."

Penny swam around and saw the worm had a hook in him, attached to a fishing line that went up out of the water to a fishing rod held by a man in a boat. She could see other men catching fish and putting more worms on hooks to catch more fish.

Penny didn't like this at all, and she dipped back under the water to tell her friends.

"The poor worm is definitely having a terrible day," she said. "We should help him."

And from that moment on, any time a worm said mean things, Penny first tried to understand why it was not in a good mood.

Penny always tried to be the bigger fish.

THE CHATTERBOX

1. Do mean people make you angry?
2. Do you sometimes get baited by what they say to you and want to bite back with mean words?
3. How does that make you feel?
4. If you get baited and start to get angry, how do you feel afterward?

5. If you knew no one else believed their mean words and that the person saying them was having a terrible day, would you feel differently about the situation?
6. What would you advise Penny to do next time—take the bait and bite the worm on the hook, or not take it personally, and be the bigger fish?
7. What should you do in situations like that?
8. Do you think it will be easy to remain calm when someone is mean to you?
9. Would you rather be a minnow and take the bait, even if it is easier, or be the bigger fish and not get caught, even if it is harder?

THE BIGGER FISH

```
M F D O T C Z B D C J B A C F
Z H Q F G L O O F L P V V M O
T E O M I R V M S T A Q S J K
O L V T N V U B P H P X E E U
F P Q R B N N U G L O M J D J
G Y U O E A D D O U A C P F T
Y Q B U S W E G O U D I K V N
R P C B T W R X D Y E O N E M
S D C L W O S V I E F W O T D
A E A E J W T T L M I O K D W
P N W A C O A W Z N A R J L A
L E G U M R N U K N N M U Z D
G M A R C S D M U G T S X S L
D P Z C Y T M B A I T I N G O
E B B Q E I O B M E Q F I S H
```

understand	complain	defiant	best
baiting	shocked	trouble	fish
peace	worms	angry	help
worst	good		

8

HUGS AND PROTEIN BARS

I n my earnest efforts to become the best parent I could be, I tried to research everything—*be* everything—for my kids. It took me just over a decade to learn that perhaps I had been overthinking it. Maybe our job is not as hard as we believe it should be.

My daughter is an avid, competitive swimmer. And I have a friend with an older son on the same swim team. I cannot tell you how much of our lives have been spent with chlorine overwhelming our senses, and adrenaline, too, as we watch our little angels "build character."

It was a challenge—encouraging them, taking them to meets, timing them, filming them, caring about countless stats, remembering races, and trying to justify to ourselves why dropping 0.1 seconds after three months of training is a worthwhile achievement. But at the same time, it was an excellent outlet for the kids, and we supported them in the way we believed they wanted.

But there was a moment at one of the meets—a conversation between my friend and her son—that changed my entire perspective towards parenting.

He'd just finished a race, done okay, and came over to his mom to touch base and ensure she'd videoed his turns.

Foolishly, not only had she videoed his turns, she had opinions about them, voiced them, coached him on how he could save another 0.1 seconds off his personal best, and then waited for him to express profound gratitude for sharing her thoughts and enlightening him with parental wisdom.

"Can you not coach me" was the response she got.

So, she gave him a hug and a protein bar, and off he went, back to his friends.

She vented for a minute, then we hunkered down, ready for another two hours of brain death before the next 33.2 seconds of pure vicarious validation, and we reflected on our purpose here on Earth.

It wasn't to high-five them if they did great; they have their friends for that.

It wasn't to talk them off the ledge if they did poorly; he'd made that clear.

It wasn't to coach them; he'd made that clear, too

Nor was it to not care.

Was it to give them a protein bar and a hug? Was that it?

And that's when it dawned on me.

What they want from us has nothing to do with whether they did well; it is to feed and hug them *regardless* of their success.

Between friends, teachers, coaches, peers, and their own thinking, our kids will get all the coaching they will ever need to succeed. But none of it matters—none of it will *stick*—if they don't know that at the end of the day, they will be loved, fed, and supported emotionally, regardless of what kind of day they had.

If our children know that the love and care we provide is not results-driven—not a reflection of their performance—we reach through the magic mirror. They will become confident adults and get all the coaching they need from the rest of the world.

So, as we bring this book to a close, I would like to conclude with this simple message of support and hope.

One day, this phase will be done. It may not feel like it, but it's a fact. It will end. If you do nothing else, give your kids a hug and a protein bar, *regardless* of how well they've done. A secure kid is an open mind, and a secure kid is a reflection of a secure parent who is confident that you will eventually get through this.

My friend's son now works in the financial sector, and I talked with them both while writing this book.

"Yeah," he said many times. "I remember those days. It feels like a lifetime ago."

We got through it, and so will you, with a hug, a protein bar, and a few stories to help us along the way.

HUGS AND PROTEIN BARS

```
G S U P P O R T C T X U T E U
A G R A T I T U D E A E D L Z
K S O H N T C B M L Y B K O L
E K O C O N F I D E N T X V K
B C E T G B D D Z E P D Z E W
S Q O N U M O Q O Q N L Y D E
C C T M C C H A R A C T E R X
D P N C P O O X J G E I A H P
S L U U V E U R V U Y M H Q R
I U J R V S T R J P S B U I E
R B C N P E S I A I X T G Y S
E E L C D O F W T G H W I M S
O S R H E Y S M I I I Q F F D
Z T S W P S E E R M V N R G Y
S K U G Z U S T S Y J E G T C
```

competitive	character	encouraging	best
confident	support	purpose	hug
success	justify	express	
swim	gratitude	loved	

❤

I hope you found this book enjoyable and that it has been a helpful tool for your family in addressing anger issues with your kids. If you found this book valuable, your review would be greatly appreciated.

www.ingramcontent.com/pod-product-compliance
Lightning Source LLC
Chambersburg PA
CBHW020327130626
46549CB00003B/1047